ems should be returned on or before the last date
hown below. Items not already requested by other
orrowers may be renewed in person, in writing or by
elephone. To renew, please quote the number on the
arcode label. To renew on line a PIN is required.
his can be requested at your local library.
enew online @ **www.dublincitypubliclibraries.ie**
ines charged for overdue items will include postage
ıcurred in recovery. Damage to or loss of items will be
harged to the borrower.

Following the

PINK
RIBBON
PATH

First published in 2018 by

columbaBOOKS

23 Merrion Square
Dublin 2, Ireland
www.columbabooks.com

ISBN: 978-1-78218-348-8

Set in Freight Text Pro 10/13
Cover and book design by Alba Esteban | Columba Books

Printed by ScandBook, Sweeden

Following the

PINK
RIBBON
PATH

MARY REDMOND USSHER

columba
BOOKS

For all on this path
with love and hope

Mary Redmond Ussher

CONTENTS

*To aid Loving Mind–Body Awareness and Christian Meditation the audio
of these chapters is available on: http://pinkribbonpath.com/meditations

O woman

O woman clothed in the sun
with the moon at your feet
crown of twelve stars on your head
pink ribbon at your breast
queen of hope
queen of healing
queen of peace
pray for us

....
MRU

FOREWORD

"A single sunbeam is enough
to drive away many shadows."

....

St. Francis of Assisi

Through the pain and suffering of hardship and illness, there can emerge a beam of light. Over time, that light can become increasingly brighter until, eventually, it can illuminate your life in a wholly new way. The Pink Ribbon Path is a path of light born of darkness, finding its catalyst in illness but finding its expression in a life of renewed joy, wholeness and purpose. Illness does not have to define us. We can be ill, yet whole.

The Pink Ribbon Path is a path of many paradoxical blessings, blessings that would not be as great were it not for the adversity which creates them. My mother kept the following quotation close to her: "Don't try to mend a broken heart. God loves it broken...The atom releases energy only when it is split. The broken heart and its prayer 'in extremis' has a tremendous force."[1] To be human is to be vulnerable. To be ill is to be at our most vulnerable and therefore at our most human. And that is precisely when we can find our greatest strength, when the broken heart can find its 'tremendous force'. This 'tremendous force' means that, even though we

1.Unknown. I have been unable to trace this quotation.

may face a most difficult reality, we need not be overcome by it. Julian of Norwich wrote: "He did not say: 'You will not be troubled'; 'You will not be laboured'; 'You will not be afflicted'. But He did say 'You will not be overcome'."[2] These words represent the heartfelt essence of the Pink Ribbon Path: the human spirit can shine strongly and with love even through the greatest adversity. As Teresa of Avila wrote: "In the midst of sickness, the heart may be offered."[3]

To Live, To Love, To Leave a Legacy

When I was a child, I asked my mother what the meaning of life was. She answered: "To live, to love and to leave a legacy", words of advice that her father had also given to her when she was young.

Her legacy has been far-reaching and includes her extensive legal and academic work in employment law. In early 2018, a new edition of one of her legal works was updated by Desmond Ryan and published, in tribute to my mother, as *Redmond on Dismissal* (Bloomsbury). Outside of her legal work, my mother was actively involved in the charity sector in Ireland. In 1999, she instigated a national charity called The Wheel, which brings together the community and voluntary sectors. The Wheel promotes the idea of 'active citizenship' and has played a key role in encouraging a more participatory democracy in Ireland.

---

2. P. 25 of original Pink Ribbon Path (PRP).
3. This was from a diary entry my mum made, quoting Teresa of Avila. However, my mum did not give the source.

But her father's advice to her ultimately led my mother to fulfil another far-reaching aspect of her legacy and from the most personal possible circumstances. Indeed, it was the careful and kind hospice care that her father, Sean Redmond, received at the end of his life which led my mother to found, in 1986, The Irish Hospice Foundation, a charity which campaigns for best practice in end of life care. The Irish Hospice Foundation has played a huge role in bringing hospice care forward in Ireland over the last three decades. In 1986, there were only three hospices in Ireland, today there are nine. Whereas then only one specific area in Dublin had access to hospice home care services, now this is a national service which anyone at end of life can avail of. And, at a local level, the Irish Hospice Foundation has helped oversee annual Sunflower Days and Coffee Mornings that have raised over €35 million for local hospices. My mother's work in The Irish Hospice Foundation was part of a dream, a vision, that no one in Ireland should go without dignified end of life care. My mother had a special capacity to envision change. As she once said: "As anyone with a dream will tell you, not only does it never go away, you see it, you can touch it and you talk about it at every opportunity."[4]

Those achievements represent the core of my mother's legacy and, in 2014, she received an honorary doctorate from Trinity College Dublin for these contributions. As her son, however, I witnessed what was, for me, a different kind of legacy and a much more personal one. And that legacy came from how

4. Inaugural Mary Redmond Day Lecture, St Francis' Hospice, 13th February 2004.

she lived and how she loved, those two other aspects of her father's advice, over the six years of her having breast cancer. Through those years until her passing in April 2015, I saw her truly live to the fullest. Not in the sense of packing a whirlwind of activities into every day but rather by living out fully the 'quiet miracle of the ordinary'. I could see clearly how a sense of the deep preciousness of each moment took root in my mother, despite the physical pain of illness. As she wrote: "Help me to accept my everyday / just as it is, / the quirky pains and aches all over, / tenderness in hands and feet. / This, my everyday / I lay before you as it is."[5] This acceptance freed her heart, allowing it not just to accept, but to love her everyday. It also allowed her to be fully present in sharing a cup of tea with a loved one, in taking in the springtime sunlight, in gardening and painting. And, most strikingly, this acceptance freed her to be fully present for friends and family, to be the kind and listening ear, to leave others feeling better than before they met her, and to be a loving sister, wife and mum.

My mother called the strength to live in this way the 'Pink Ribbon Path', and it stemmed from her own experience, from her practice of meditation and from a wide range of inspiring authors whom she read in the early years of her illness. After some years, she drew together her own writings and these different sources of inspiration and, in 2013, *The Pink Ribbon Path* was first published under my mother's married name, Ussher.

My mother passed away, surrounded by family, on April

---

5. Original PRP, p. 44.

6th, 2015. Two days before that, I had my last conversation with her. On that day, I told her how beautifully she had walked the Pink Ribbon Path, and I promised her that I would do my best to ensure that it would live on. The book you now hold in your hands is the fulfilment of that promise. This time the book is published under her maiden name and the name by which she was better known, Redmond. The book contains new reflections on walking this spiritual path, from a range of contributors who have been touched by the Pink Ribbon Path in some way, all of whom knew my mother personally. I wish to convey my heartfelt gratitude to the authors of these new reflections for their most thoughtful contributions, which show that the Pink Ribbon Path is a universal path that transcends any one person's experience.

For me, this book represents the completion of my mother's legacy. It combines poignantly her life-long sense of care for the vulnerable (as embodied previously in her work in setting up the Irish Hospice Foundation and the Wheel) with her own spirituality of strength, a spirituality which stemmed, paradoxically, from her own vulnerability during the years of illness. From that position, she wrote this book as a 'wounded healer', with the beautiful message to us all that "we can be ill, yet whole".[6] *Following the Pink Ribbon Path* contains a universal message of finding meaning in suffering, of living with joy despite the possible limitations of the body, and of taking up willingly the choice we always have of radiating love, both inwardly and outwardly.

---

6. Original PRP, p.10.

I feel privileged to have witnessed my mother walking this spiritual path. I saw, in reality, what the heart of the Pink Ribbon Path is all about. And I would now like to try to capture the essence of that path for you. I am aware of my limitations in doing so and I only hope that I can do it justice.

Surrender

"Today more than any other day I see myself taking up the Cross of Christ and carrying it. I will do so with a smile."

....

June 10th, 2009.

These words, written by my mother on her first day of chemotherapy, became symbolic of how she came to live in the years that followed. I will never forget how intensely beautiful and radiant her smile remained, often in the face of great suffering. Early into her treatment, I remember her learning to smile at the grey, wispy hairs that had started to grow on her head and, later, proudly displaying her new 'hairstyle', which forced her to be in the world with great vulnerability. For me, that new hairstyle, in time, became the most beautiful hair, representing the inherent strength that living with vulnerability necessarily requires.

That vulnerability also focuses the mind on what really matters, and that is the very business of living and the quiet miracle of the everyday. Early on, my mother made a decision not to 'participate in her illness'. By this she meant that she decided not to let the 'narrative of illness' take over her life, choosing not to get caught up in a reality where 'being sick' was the predominant output. Instead, she wrote to herself: "Decide to fill your world with joy. Anticipate joyful events each day and ponder them in the evening."[7] This is not to deny the reality of illness or the need for careful consideration of treatment and management of symptoms. Rather, this is about making the conscious decision that our daily lives need not, as far as we are able, be weighed down by the burden of illness.

That this was possible was also because she surrendered to God. She wrote: "When a diagnosis of serious illness arrives, we are challenged in what we believe. God's face seems hidden. As a lawyer, I was used to solving problems no matter how difficult. This was a problem I knew I could not solve. And so I placed my hands in God's. It was 'over to Him'."[8] To leave all in God's hands relieves us of a large psychological burden, that of trying to solve what we cannot solve, and frees us to focus on positivity and on love, both of which are key. This way of approaching life also still allows for playfulness and humour. Illness cannot deny the right of both to be in our lives. My mother had a great sense of fun and, if anything, this increased over the Pink Ribbon Path years. This sense of playfulness even led her to write an imaginative and beauti-

7. Personal Diary (2009).
8. Notes in preparation for a talk my mum gave during her tour of America, November/December 2014.

ful children's book about Irish fairies and leprechauns called *Marlena The Fairy Princess*.

Early on in my mother's treatment, she came across an anonymous poem in the Oratory of the hospital. It was called 'The Tandem Bike Ride'.[9] In the poem, the author is seated at the front of the bike and Jesus is at the back. Both are pedalling but as the author is at the front, he has control over the direction in which they go. However, at a certain point, the author switches places with Jesus, allowing Jesus to guide the author of the poem into new and unexpected directions:

> ...it seemed as though life was rather like a bike ride,
> but it was a tandem bike,
> and I noticed that Christ
> was in the back helping me pedal.
> I don't know just when it was
> That he suggested we change places,
> But life has not been the same since.

My mother said of this poem: "I found exactly that happening to me, that at a certain stage, particularly when I felt I have no answers to this anymore, somehow, imperceptibly, I changed places in the same way."[10] Illness can teach us to let go of trying to control our lives and instead let the Spirit guide us, and this can take us to places we would never otherwise

---

9. Original PRP, p.91.
10. American Interview, November 2014, from the Celtic Show with Jonathan Kiger.

have gone. The author of the poem was taken to "...people with gifts that I needed, / gifts of healing, / acceptance / and joy", and these too are the gifts of the Pink Ribbon Path. The road might seem to be closed to us, but surrendering allows us to find a way forward which will lead us to a whole new kind of life, and one that we would never have had otherwise. It allows us, as my mother often used to say, to wear life like a loose garment. And to take the back seat on the tandem bike also gives us strength. My mother wrote: "I'm on the tandem bike. Jesus rides before me, I trust in him. If I waver, I hear him say 'Pedal!' So I do."[11] And the time to ride that bike comes round, again and again. Early on a morning of chemotherapy, my mother wrote this short poem:

"Outside my window/ winter flowering cherry tree / gradually dawns / pink-dotting the bare mountain / can't delay for beauty / I've a tandem bike to ride"[12]

Meditation

"At meditation, I thought when breathing in and out of the words: 'O moment beautiful, O moment made divine. O present divine. Present made divine. O divine present. Gift that is divine."

....

November 12th, 2009.

11.Personal Diary (2010).
12.Personal Diary (2010).

"Meditation leads the mind into a free zone that is not touched by illness."[13] These words of my mother speak to the need, when we are ill, of having a space in our lives in which the continuum of illness can be broken. In the early months of diagnosis, my mother found that space through the practice of meditation.

She was in particular soon drawn to the practice of Christian Mindfulness, a form of meditation developed by the Benedictine monk, John Main (1926-1982). This kind of meditation involves repeating a mantra, silently and calmly to oneself. The mantra that is recommended is 'Maranatha' which is the Aramaic word for 'Come, Lord'. She came to describe her practice of this as follows: "Personally, I spend thirty minutes in meditation, morning and evening. It becomes an intrinsic part of your life. You sit quietly, saying the mantra, maranatha, on the in-breath, and your mind grows quieter and quieter. It is literally seeing things with a new vision, introducing the newness of the Gospels into your time and space. In peace, solitude and the absence of words, something changes in you. You find yourself resting in the Lord, and who wouldn't want to do that? A friend of mine says that in meditation he inhales the Spirit in his in-breath. It is literally 'inspirare', breathing in the Spirit."[14]

To meditate like this is to rest in a powerful and divine Love which suffuses the present moment. In this way, silence becomes a kind of 'heavenly gift'. In light of this, my mother also wrote: "I am aware that in this moment I am not alone. I

---

13. Personal Diary (2013).
14. From Credo, Personal Testimonies of Faith (Edited by John Quinn), p.140.

am still in His silence. I am aware that God is with me. My Lord and my God. You are the Way, the Truth and the Light. You are with me, this little child, in this precious moment. Mary, my mother, is blessing me. You are comforting me, I can feel your arms around me. I am still and I am aware of You with me, here. I love You. I know that You love me. I am aware of your powerful Love. O blissful moment, O triune God."[15] Thomas Merton, a Cistercian monk who wrote much on contemplative prayer and whose writings were a great source of inspiration for my mother, said that solitude and silence could lead you to a heavenly light, a heavenly light which would resonate deep within: "I, Solitude, am thine own self...I, Silence, am thy Amen."[16] Resting in the Divine present, this 'Amen', can be a source of great daily renewal, during which time the narrative of sickness is transcended. In an unpublished poem, my mother wrote:

"On my break / after five rounds of chemotherapy / hands numb / bone-flares / ears ringing / I sit still / light a candle / close my eyes / and listen / for a breath / for a breeze."

This stillness can envelop us, wounded as we are, with Love and can interrupt the continuum of illness.

This kind of meditation also transforms the rest of the day, allowing us to focus on and honour each part of it. My mother's spirituality was greatly influenced by the work of Fr John Sullivan (1861-1933). He wrote: "Take life in instalments, this

---

15.Personal Diary (2009).

16.Recorded in my mum's diary. From a poem by Thomas Merton, 'Song: If you Seek....', published in Emblems of a Season of Fury (New Directions, 1963).

one day now. At least let this be a good day. Be always beginning. Let the past go. Now let me do whatever I have power to do. The Saints were always beginning. That is how they became saints."

Shifting our attention to how we live this very day allows us to create our life more mindfully, weaving a tapestry of days well lived, one after the other. Narrowing our focus more towards the present also allows us to cope better. My mother wrote: "Face any fears that surface in your mind and know that they are about the future which has not, and may never happen, and reassure yourself that, should they transpire, you will apply the same coping skills then as now."[17] If we can cope well with our present, then we are automatically preparing well for the future, and whatever it may bring.

The practice of meditation also allows us to see each day with fresh eyes. My mother's poem, 'Hearing the Flowers', which playfully reworks a famous Simon & Garfunkel song, speaks to this:

> Slow down
> Don't move too fast
> Want to make
> Each moment last
> Want to hear
> The flowers grow
> Feel their rhythm
> In my soul[18]

---

17. Personal Diary (2013).
18. Original PRP, p.89.

Meditation can instil a love of Creation. My mother often used to say that every day, every moment, every nanosecond, was so precious.

My mother described practising meditation as being akin to 'entering the Heart-room'. It is a time and space in which to be compassionate and gentle with yourself. "Love yourself, something most of us do not do, at all, ever. Do so now."[19] And it is also a place where that love you bring to yourself can meet an even greater, Divine love. On the Pink Ribbon Path, meditation is a practice of sitting in and with that powerful love. It is, as my mother wrote, "the now of loving, of meditating."[20]

I used to sit most evenings with my mother in meditation. These were the most precious times for me. Sometimes, I'd open my eyes and just take a peak at her, so grateful to be alive with her, in that present moment, and in her presence. My abiding memory is of her sitting with a smile, 'ensconced' fully in the love of the moment.

The Pink Ribbon Path is Our Human Path

One of the poems in this book is called *'Summa Cum Laude'*.[21] In Latin, this means 'With the Greatest Honour' and it is a phrase normally applied to those who graduate from univer-

---

19.Personal Diary (2013).
20.Personal Diary (2010).
21.Original PRP, p. 99.

sity having done well in their degree. In this poem, my mother speaks of the process of 'graduating' *summa cum laude* from the 'school of blessings', which is, paradoxically, the school of cancer. The poem reads:

> If breast cancer returns
> I'll be a postgraduate
> at a school I call
> the school of blessings
> I was nervous
> when matriculating
> but Mary led me to her Son
>
> His love made me thrive
> enlarged my heart
> to the whole universe
> when I graduated
> neither pain nor death
> held me in thrall
> whoever would have thought
> cancer could be God's megaphone.

Later, my mother wrote a different poem, unpublished until now, and which was found among her belongings in hospital. It speaks to the words you have just read:

I am a graduate
summa cum laude
of the school of suffering
aka the College of Cancer...
I cry to you
summa cum laude
we are all in this together.

We are all in this together. These words speak to the universality of human suffering, to the fact that we are all mortal. And yet these words also speak to the fact that there is a path, a way to find light in and among the harsh realities that we all must face at some point, and that when we find that path, we are truly on a process of 'graduating *summa cum laude*'. The College of Cancer is but one way that can lead us to that path, one way that hardship can become 'God's megaphone'. When we walk that path and attend to our own suffering with compassion, we come into contact with the suffering which we all share. This is what enlarges our heart and expands our love towards others. This is what reifies each and every day we have and what allows us to sense the preciousness of each moment.

The College of Cancer is symbolic of our human journey. To walk the Pink Ribbon Path is to walk with grace and dignity the most human of paths. It is to find that sunbeam described by St. Francis of Assisi and which my mother also described in a talk she gave in 2013: "What a blessing too that each of us carries that single sunbeam in our heart-rooms, radiating love and light, reminding us that this world is but a stage on our real pilgrimage."[22] My mother's cry to you is to find that sunbeam. It will sustain you on this path.

---

22. Dr. Mary Redmond, Annual Hospice Lecture, Feb 2013.

The Opening of the Lotus:
The Blessings of the Pink Ribbon Path

The Pink Ribbon Path brings many blessings. For my mother, although she was on 'sick leave' from work, it turned out to be a time filled with joy and discovery. It was a time of discovery, richness, sharing in the Cross and learning to pray without the need for words; to be, not do. It was a time of learning that God is within us, of the divine present, and of sensing the strength of God's love for all creation. The Pink Ribbon Path can reorder and rebalance our lives in ways that enrich them beyond words. What might have seemed the end of the road, can just be a turn, a bend, a new direction which will take us somewhere full of unexpected gifts and blessings.

One year into the Pink Ribbon Path, my mother wrote of the blessings that had emerged: "It has been a time of the worst imaginable findings, of turning to God (I am in Your hands now), of finding the child Jesus in the temple, of gradually building a mosaic of spiritual friends, of seeking and finding and loving, of discovering the true meaning of family, husband and son, mother, sisters, brother, of learning to go into the castle of silence and stillness and knowing You are God, of praying by the fingertips and never letting go....O how much squandered time before all this. Slowly came trust, hope, courage, patience, longing, sweetness, Christian meditation / mindfulness, indispensable allies. What a personal discovery, the sacrament of Now. Looking back, the lotus flower was closed, submerged in cloudy water, one year ago. Now, how changed it is, petals expanding, increasing, slowly, opening. Water clear, reflecting the sun. Giving and receiving its blessings. Now St Paul's words can be lived: 'Don't be anxious; instead, give thanks in all your prayers and petitions and make your requests known to God. And God's peace which is beyond all understanding will keep your hearts and minds in Christ Jesus'."[23]

It was a huge honour for me to witness my mother walk this path and a huge blessing to sit with her in silence, 'the now of loving, of meditating'. I hope that the Pink Ribbon Path will unfold for you, like the slowly expanding petals of the lotus flower, towards that single and radiant sunbeam which can be found in the heart of each one of us.

Patrick Ussher
Dublin, September 2018

---

23. Personal Diary (2014).

INTRODUCTION

When a woman is diagnosed with breast cancer, life becomes a whirl of new information, it takes on a new dimension, revolving around scans, bloods, markers, infusions, and side effects, of which the most dreaded is hair loss. Too easily overlooked in all of this is the force within us with its wonderful message: we can be ill, yet whole. Inner wholeness was something I discovered and reclaimed during my treatment for breast cancer, and it has become for me a true ally, not just in my illness but in all of my life.

This book is an invitation to women with breast cancer to consider trying to re-find that wholeness, as I did, on the Pink Ribbon Path. It is a path for healing, for living, for hope, a journey which once embarked upon becomes a daily joy.

From the time I joined the cancer community in 2009 I kept a journal in which I wrote down personal reflections and transcribed prayers or words that I found inspiring. This I did during the different stages of breast cancer: on diagnosis, during treatment; after treatment; and after that, when life and living became renewed sources of profound joy. During this time, the Pink Ribbon Path slowly emerged, a spiritual path enabling rediscovery of inner strength and thus of undivided wholeness. This spiritual flourishing means meeting with awareness whatever challenges arise. Whatever the circumstances, whatever the outlook, you are not alone in your illness. The Spirit is walking with you.

Wholeness and resourcefulness encourage transcendence in relation to what is so often feared by cancer patients: recurrence of the illness. This book, I hope, will speak equally to women whose breast cancer has returned. I pray that, for all women, it may be a reminder, alongside medical treatment and care, to seek the treasure within.

The Pink Ribbon Path reflects the emotions I felt at each stage of the journey: the fear when out of the blue there was a diagnosis of breast cancer; the hope that medical treatment would be effective; the new and different fears and anxieties that followed treatment; then, the slow evolution of spiritual flourishing, come what may. Through these emotions I found myself growing 'downwards', towards my inner, true self. Perspectives changed.

Being on any path needs discipline, although once that path becomes a way of joyful living, time is made, willingly, for the daily journey. A transforming event for me on the Pink Ribbon Path was encountering Christian Meditation. Dom John Main OSB summarised its effect well: 'When we meditate, not only do we stand back from the individual operations of our being, but we begin to learn to find a wholly new ground to stand on. We discover a rootedness of being. The rootedness is not just in ourselves, but we discover ourselves rooted in God. Rooted in God who is Love.'

Christian Meditation is an act of love. It does not produce bells and whistles during our silence. But over time we find love growing in our heart, we become lovingly attentive to our selves in our everyday, just as we are, however tired or weak. At the same time, we reach out to others compassionately. And as we know that God has sent his Spirit to dwell in us, we become open, rooted, to his Being. This rootedness or wholeness brings greater clarity, and forgiveness of anything that may stand in the way of his Love. It facilitates a choice of responses to events rather than reactions to them. Anyone going through major illness will know how often their reactions are driven by fear.

Hazrat Inayat Khan says that the mind is the surface of the heart, the heart the depth of the mind. The Pink Ribbon Path is the path of the heart. If you have been diagnosed with breast cancer, whether for the first time or otherwise, I hope you will regard this book as a companion on successive stages of the journey, using the readings for reflection at each stage, perhaps composing and adding your own. Needless to say, you may join the Path whatever the stage of your illness: the journey inwards may begin at any time. A Loving Mind–Body Awareness, narrated by Sue Norton, who I thank, follows the four stages in the book. This stopping and becoming lovingly aware of our mind and body is integral to the journey, from the beginning. It is as much a part of the Path as the two daily meditation sessions to which we listen with the ear of the heart.

May Loving Awareness and Christian Meditation accompany you daily at every stage of your life.

Mary Redmond Ussher

Diagnosis

Mother

How powerfully the Spirit
worked in you
dear mother
for I could not have known
anything was wrong
Yet upstairs while you prayed
I noticed an apparently
innocuous change
in my breast
and made a call

....
MRU

66

But now ... the hurricane has come, and you feel you are being shaken by a force that could uproot century-old trees. You feel this from without and from within. But you must remain confident, for your Faith and your Love cannot be uprooted, nor can you be blown from your way ...

Contra spem in spem! – live in certain hope, against all hope. Rely on that firm rock which will save you and help you on.

You spoke about the scenes in the life of Jesus which moved you most: when he brought peace and health to those whose bodies and souls were racked with pain ... You were inspired – you went on – seeing him cure leprosy, restore sight to the blind, heal the paralytic at the pool: the poor beggar forgotten by everybody. You are able to contemplate Him as He was, so pro - foundly human, so close at hand!

—Well! Jesus continues being the same as then.

St Josemaría Escrivá, Extracts from *Furrow*

Take My Hand

I am being asked to carry
a heavy cross
Dearest Father
I am your little child
I am being asked to carry
a heavy cross
Dearest Father
Take my hand
I have never needed you so much

....
MRU

Out of the depths I cry to you, O Lord!
O Lord, hear my voice!
Let your ears be attentive
to the voice of my pleas for mercy!
I wait for the Lord, my soul waits,
and in his word I hope;
my soul waits for the Lord
more than watchmen for the morning,
more than watchmen for the morning.

Psalm 130:1–2, 5–6

Likewise the Spirit helps us in our weakness.
For we do not know what to pray for as we
ought, but the Spirit himself intercedes for
us with groanings too deep for words. And
he who searches hearts knows what is the
mind of the Spirit, because the Spirit
intercedes for the saints according to the will
of God. And we know that God causes all
things to work together for good to those
who love God, to those who are called
according to this purpose.

St Paul, Romans 8: 26–8

"

Thus says the Lord who made you,
who formed you from the womb and
will help you:
Fear not.

Isaiah 44:2

"

Jesus did not come to explain away suffering or to remove
it. He came to fill it with his presence.

Paul Claudel

"

God is our refuge and strength,
a very present help in trouble.
Therefore we will not fear though the
earth gives way,
though the mountains be moved into
the heart of the sea;
though its waters roar and foam,
though the mountains tremble at its swelling.

Psalm 46:1–3

Love

Husband, lover, partner, best friend
Never has our one-ness
been so sacramental
In sickness now
our union
Cover me with your love

....
MRU

Faith, hope and love. Her faith she expressed daily in her actions; she never ceased to have hope for a better future; and love....she was surrounded by love, and loved her loved ones with all her heart.

Fortitude, good humour and a sense of fun, despite all; eyes sparkling, the smile ready, despite all.

The greater the love, the greater the grief. I have her in my thoughts continually. The love is the link between us still.

Patrick D.L. Ussher

Calming the Storm

I see Jesus with his disciples in the boat
beset by a gale and breaking waves.
They wake him saying, 'Master, do you not
care? We are going down.'
He orders the sea to be calm
and the wind to drop.
Then he says to them,
'Why are you so frightened?
How is it that you have no faith?'
The disciples were filled with awe.
I believe Jesus is in this boat, with me.
Lord Jesus, I trust in you.
Help me. Calm my fears.

....
MRU

66

Pray, Hope and Don't Worry.

....
St Pio of Pietrelcina

66

Do not be afraid!
Open the doors to Christ.
God works in the concrete and personal
affairs of each one of us.

....
Blessed John Paul II

66

Let not your hearts be troubled. Believe in
God; believe also in me. ... I am the way, the
truth and the life.

....
John 14:1, 6

> He did not say,
> 'You will not be troubled:
> you will not be laboured;
> you will not be afflicted.'
> But he did say,
> 'You will not be overcome.'

Julian of Norwich

> Jesus said, 'Come to me, all who labour and are heavy laden, and I will give you rest. Take my yoke upon you, and learn from me; for I am gentle and lowly in heart, and you will find rest for your souls. For my yoke is easy, and my burden is light.'

Matthew 11:28–30

Prayer

Father
thank you
for the precious gift
of my son
may he
know your love
be strong
as you are strong
endure
with courage and with faith
the news
he heard today

....
MRU

As [Jesus] passed by, he saw a man blind from birth. And his disciples asked him, 'Rabbi, who sinned, this man or his parents, that he was born blind?' Jesus answered, 'It was not that this man sinned, or his parents, but that the works of God might be displayed in him.'

Jesus then healed his blindness.

John 9:2–3

Abide in me, and I in you. ... If you abide in me, and my words abide in you, ask whatever you wish, and it will be done for you.

John 15:4, 7

This man lives in one light with God, and therefore there is not in him either suffering or the passage of time, but an unchanging eternity. From this man, truly, all wonderment has been taken away, and all things are essentially present in him.

Therefore nothing new will come to him out of future events or accidents, for he dwells always anew in a now without ceasing.

Meister Eckhart Sermon 2

Child-Adult

Ease my sensitivities Lord
about people and what
may be imparted
concerning me.
At times like these
I feel my fragility
how utterly
I depend on you.
Child-Adult
may I be child alone
renewing each day
the newness of the day.

....
MRU

"

When you say a situation or person is hopeless, you are slamming the door in the face of God.

Charles L. Allen

"

Ask and it will be given to you; seek and you will find; knock, and it will be opened to you. For everyone who asks receives, and the one who seeks finds, and to the one who knocks it will be opened. Or which one of you, if his son asks him for bread, will give him a stone? Or if he asks for a fish, will give him a serpent? If you then, who are evil, know how to give good gifts to your children, how much more will your Father who is in heaven give good things to those who ask Him! ...

The gate is narrow and the way is hard that leads to life.

Matthew 7:7–11, 14

Now

May I be aware
of you
in-dwelling
may the sacrament of
the present moment
make past past
future fiction
and break the continuum
of illness

....
MRU

"

I wish you could convince yourself that God is often nearer in times of illness and weakness than when we are in a perfect state of health.

Bro. Lawrence of the Resurrection

"

Asking in Jesus' name means entering into him, living by him, being one with him in love and faith. If he is in us by faith, in love, in grace, in his Spirit, then our petition arises from the centre of our being which is himself, and if all our petition and desire is gathered up and fused in him and his Spirit, then the Father hears us. Then our petition becomes simple and straightforward, harmonious, sober and unpretentious. Then what St Paul says in the letter to the Romans applies to us: we do not know how to pray as we ought but the Spirit himself intercedes for us praying the one prayer, 'Abba! Father!' He longs for that from which the Spirit and Jesus have proceeded: he longs for God, he asks God for God, on our behalf he asks of God. Everything is included and contained in this prayer ... [If we pray in this way] we shall see that God really answers our prayer, in one way or another.

Karl Rahner SJ

Totus Tuus [All Yours]

I know Lord
if I live
this moment
and the next
and the next
with you
I can cope

....
MRU

What Cannot Cancer Do

It cannot cripple love,
It cannot shatter hope,
It cannot corrode faith,
It cannot eat away peace,
It cannot destroy confidence,
It cannot kill friendship,
It cannot shut out memories,
It cannot silence courage,
It cannot reduce eternal life,
It cannot quench the Spirit,
It cannot lessen the power
of the Resurrection.

....

Fr Harry Behan

How different it was to read the Pink Ribbon Path five years after publication. By 2018, not only had the wonderful author, Mary, died, but I too had come through serious cancer.

The lovely poem by Fr Harry Behan gives me great comfort and courage. It is true that cancer can do a lot of things to a person, but there is so much that it has no power over.

My simple encouragement for anyone facing cancer is to accept that while life's 'GPS' might have brought you to a place you had never planned to go, nor wished to be in, you can say "This too will pass and I will cope". This focus is not about battling cancer, or fighting against the disease, or being 'positive' – language I detest. It is simply about being: taking the medicine, seeing what the joy is in every day and seeking ways to build your resilience – for me it was my children and a daily walk on the West Pier in Dun Laoghaire.

Cancer didn't break Mary's spirit and it didn't break mine. Remembering Mary Redmond, this poem made me smile.

Sharon Foley,
CEO of the Irish Hospice Foundation

O shepherd of souls,
O first of words,
Through which we all were created,
may it please you, may it please:
free us from our fear
and fragility.

....
Hildegard of Bingen

All things contribute to good for those who love God ... assure your soul that, if it loves God, everything will be converted to good. And although you may not see the means by which this good will happen to you, be assured that it will happen ... [God] has protected you up to the present moment; just remain firmly in the hands of His providence and He will help you in all situations and at those times when you find yourself unable to walk, He will carry you. What should you fear, my dearest daughter, since you belong to God who has so strongly assured us that for those who love Him all things turn into happiness. Do not think of what may happen tomorrow, because the same eternal Father who takes care of you today, will take care of you tomorrow and forever.

....
St Francis de Sales

Treatment

The Memorare

Remember, O Most Gracious Virgin Mary,
that never was it known that anyone who
fled to your protection, implored your
help, or sought your intercession,
was left unaided.

Inspired by this confidence, I come unto
you, O Virgin of Virgins, my Mother, to you
do I come, before you I stand, sinful and
sorrowful, fearful of what is to come,
O Mother of the Word incarnate, despise
not my petitions, but in your mercy, hear
and answer me.

Amen.

"

Be still, and know that I am God.

....
Psalm 46:10

"

Let not your hearts be troubled. Believe in God; believe also in me.

....
John 14:1

"

If you ask me for anything in my name, I will do it.

....
John 14:14

"

For I will restore health to you, and your wounds I will heal, declares the Lord.

....
Jeremiah 30:17

Starting

Thank you Father for this day,
the tears shed
at Day Centre for the first time,
prayers in the oratory,
good bloods,
vein that carried the treatment,
welcoming consultant,
nurse who looked after me,
inventors of these infusions,
other women in the bay,
kindnesses too numerous to recall,
brother-in-law who visited,
sister who drove me home,
loving husband.
The battle has begun;
your armies are within.

....
MRU

Sisters

They bake for you
Buy headscarves
Eyebrows, lashes
Paint with you
Pray for you
I know why
There's no
Patron saint
Of sisters
Because
Every sister
Is a saint

....
MRU

Dearest M – Maybe (certainly!) we are not saints. But we are sisters, linked together still and for ever, as we always have been, by the bonds of sisterhood.

You had always helped us far more than we helped you. But in your illness, we wanted you to know we were at your side as you walked with such courage along the new and challenging Pink Ribbon Path. You had the grace to let us in with our offerings. In the new language of sickness, all of these had meaning: bread, 'I love you', eyelashes, 'we are with you in this', painting, 'time with you was always precious. We know it is more precious now', lifts, 'let me help you home'...

Prayers, rising like incense, with you, for you.

You painted our canvas with the brightest of colours. It was wonderful and easy to be with you, even in the most difficult circumstances (how did you manage that? some day you will tell us). You smiled so radiantly when we met, and immediately the essence of who you are, which the cancer could never touch, took over and our time together was a precious gift, the gift you gave us.

All our love, always -

Rady, Catherine, Gerardine, Janice

The Wounded Man

I think of the parable of the Good Samaritan which Jesus told in response to the question 'Who is my Neighbour?' We are told only descriptive things about the wounded man. I like to imagine that as he lay on the ground, stripped, beaten and half dead, he asked God to help him, for only the Father could. That help came after the disappointments of the priest and the Levite respectively. But the Samaritan represented God's help, which saved the wounded man. The man was not a victim, he placed his trust in God, and that trust persevered until he was rescued.

So it is for the sick. We should place our trust firmly in our Father and never falter even if he tries us by not responding immediately.

God, in the name of your Son,
May I not
speak, act or pray
like a victim

....
MRU

We must confine ourselves to the present moment, without taking thought for the one before or the one to come.

Jean-Pierre de Caussade SJ

Little children never realise all that their words imply, but if their father or mother were to come to the throne and inherit great riches, loving their little ones more than they love themselves, they would not hesitate to give them everything they want.

St Thérèse of Lisieux, The Story of a Soul

Take life in instalments, this one day now.
At least let this be a good day.
Be always beginning.
Let the past go.
Now let me do whatever I have power to do.
The saints were always beginning.
That is how they became saints.

Worry won't mend matters.

Prayer is the greatest power on earth.

Fr John Sullivan SJ
Servant of God

We are told by some ornithologists, that as dawn breaks in Springtime, birds begin the day with a burst of song. They announce to the world that they have survived the night and are about to enjoy a new day! One of the advantages of getting older is the greater awareness that life is a wonderful and precious gift. In the words of Fr John Sullivan SJ life comes in the instalment of days. Beauty, joy and wonder can be instilled in moments which pause and then pass us by because we are distracted by the past and the future. Fr John Sullivan SJ (now Blessed John Sullivan) was one of the people who inspired Mary and influenced her. For inclusion in *The Pink Ribbon Path* she chose his reflection on "taking life in instalments, this one day now" As a Jesuit he might suggest, in addition to welcoming the new day, that time be given at its end to reflecting on how the day was spent. Time can pass almost unnoticed because of preoccupation. However, the response to time can also be one of attentiveness and presence. Each day offers opportunities for wonder at the beauty of creation, for gratitude for the love and goodness of the people who touch our lives in many different ways and for recognition in moments of suffering or uncertainty that we have the inner resources by which to respond.

For a number of decades mindfulness is a subject which has been receiving considerable recognition. For me the difference between mindfulness and contemplation can perhaps be seen in that the former stresses the importance of living in the present, the latter recognises the Presence in the present. In meeting Mary during the years of her illness it was obvious that she lived each day to the full. She lived in the present with its many dimensions and sought to leave the past and future where they belong. Being a contemplative at heart Mary was also conscious of the Presence within the present. She recognised the power of prayer in helping her to be attuned to the presence of the loving God who always accompanied her. The words from Ps 118 resonated within Mary and shone through her. "This is the day which the Lord has made, let us be glad and rejoice in it."

Sr Bernadette McMahon, Daughters of Charity

Father

Fill me with the healing power of your Spirit.
Cast out anything that should not be in me.
Mend what is broken.
Root out any unproductive cells. ...
Let the warmth of your healing love pass
through my body to make new any
unhealthy areas,
so that my body will function the way you
created it to function.
And Father, restore me to full health
in body, mind and spirit
so that I may serve you
for the rest of my life.
I ask this through Christ Our Lord
Amen.

Extract from anonymous, Prayer for Healing

This, My Everyday

Help me to accept my everyday
just as it is,
the quirky pains and aches
all over,
tenderness in hands and feet.
This, my everyday
I lay before you as it is.
Help me to love my everyday,
every moment
where I can be 'all there' with you
and 'all here'
giving myself unreservedly to this oneness.
This, my everyday
I lay before you as it is.
Thank you for this everyday,
your healing touch in every cell,
re-bodying me,
my presence to my deepest self.
This, my everyday
I lay before you as it is.

....
MRU

The power in this poem is the deep-felt 'acceptance' within it. Acceptance, in Mary's case, of all of the trappings on her most difficult cancer journey. An acceptance that allowed Mary rise above the daily frustrations of illness to a renewed sense of centredness and an ever-deepening spirituality.

I have not known in my lifetime anyone more deeply spiritual than was Mary, profoundly deep and indeed fathoms deep. The sentiments within this poem will touch many. Indeed, these sensitively expressed sentiments have touched me greatly on my own cancer journeys (and in my life generally), albeit in my stoic and less affective way.

There is a universality here: these words are bigger than a cancer journey and can be applied to any challenges that present themselves on our daily journey through life.

These verses are not just to be read. They are to be re-read and re-read again to the joyful and calming point of absorption into one's everyday life.

Thank you, Mary, firstly for the gift of you and your most valued friendship over so many years but also for the gift of this wonderful book and in particular 'This, My Everyday' – a treasure for every day of my life.

Frank Scott-Lennon, HR & Wellbeing Consultant

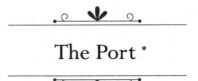

The Port *

Thank God for the port.
I no longer need to drink three pints of water
before arriving, nor soak my hands
in warm water for ten minutes.
Today I am asked to relax and lie back
so the needle can be inserted in the port.
'We'll go on three,' says the nurse.
'Deep breath in, deep breath out, that's one;
deep breath in, deep breath out, that's two;
deep breath in, here we go – well done!
Very good blood return.'
Soon she's labelling a phial of blood and
I open my eyes and say 'thank God'
and I know verily you are the Way.

MRU

*Portacath / Port catheter

Take comfort; before long God will heal you.
Raphael the Archangel to Tobias
No soul that has ever called upon my mercy
has ever been disappointed ... I am love and
mercy itself. Let no one fear to draw near to
me ... The graces of my mercy are drawn by
means of one vessel only, and that is – trust.
The more a soul trusts, the more it will receive.

St Faustina Kowalska, *quoting the words spoken to her by Jesus*

Commit your way to the Lord;
trust in him, and he will act.

Psalm 37:5

May I Be Healed

Ut videam, Domine.
I want to follow you along the road
like Bartimaeus, the blind beggar, shouting,
Son of David, Jesus, have pity on me.
I want you to hear me, to call me
as you did Bartimaeus.
Call him here you said
and the people called the blind man,
who, throwing off his cloak,
jumped up and went to you.
I want, too, to hear you call
so that, soul brimming, I may go to you
and hear your words,
what do you want me to do for you?

Bartimaeus, asked that question, said
Master, let me see again
for he had not always been blind.
Master, let me be well again, heal me,
make me as I was before, Rabbuni,
Son of David, Jesus, have pity on me.
Turn to me, as you did to Bartimaeus,
and say
Go, your faith has saved you.
And I will say
What do you want me, Lord, to do for you?

....

MRU

The heart-thumping, gut-gnawing realisation that Death is demanded of us, life will be wrenched from us, that there may be no turning back from the path of sickness, that there is no clock that can be turned back or no miracle that will restore life and hope, that pleas for a divine intervention which will dismiss this haunting fear, this not so quiet desperation, may go unanswered... These thoughts and emotions are all to be found in Mary's words written from inside that isolating, perplexing silo of terminal illness. But something deeper and less anguished also moves through these words. It is a dialogue with the God who made her. Through that discourse Mary does not drown in disappointment or clamour in self-pity but like that other Mary Mother of God whose happy life was interrupted and changed by the appearance of the Angel Gabriel, Mary finds in herself a willingness to ask of God, what can I do for you? What a turning of tables! From desperation comes transcendence, from absorbing physical and psychological pain a pathway opens to acceptance. The conscript supplicant becomes the volunteer servant. Like Heaney she can ask us still to "believe in miracles and cures and healing wells", to never give up on life but when confronted with dying, to embrace its challenges and emerge the victor willing the rest of us on from the communion of saints- as she does and does and does.

Mary McAleese, President of Ireland 1997-2011.

You Are Here

Once more I am in my bay,
needle in, bloods done,
starting the pre-meds
I introduce myself to my companions
Brian, Brenda, who's the third?
better leave her be,
it's her first day and she's in tears
her partner lingered for a while
now he's gone
I notice her long, auburn hair
hair here is rare
the book she holds
receives her tears
all round me
people are hooked up to IV lines,
some in wheelchairs, many dozing.
God is present in each one of us.
'Bidden or unbidden,
God is here.'

....
MRU

"

Teach us, good Lord,
to serve thee as thou deservest;
To give, and not to count the cost;
To fight, and not to heed the wounds;
To toil, and not to seek for rest;
To labour, and not to ask for any reward
Save that of knowing that we do thy will,
Through Jesus Christ our Lord, Amen.

St Ignatius Loyola

"

Are not two sparrows sold for a penny? And not one of them will fall to the ground apart from your Father. But even the hairs of your head are all numbered. Fear not, therefore; you are of more value than many sparrows.

Matthew 10:29–31

Needlepark

Dear chemo, travel
in top gear,
aim with the accuracy
of an Exocet,
destroy bad cells,
avoid the good,
you know by now
how welcome you are.
Triune God,
Father, Son, and Holy Spirit.
One in Three
outnumber me today
in 'Needlepark'.

....
MRU

Do not be afraid to tell Jesus that you love him, even though you may not feel that love. In this way you will compel him to come to your aid, and to carry you like a little child who is too weak to walk.

St Thérèse of Lisieux

Refuge

I am suffering
the pain of it clouds
your face, Father
I am not well enough
to go anywhere
I will go into my castle
and seek you
Your child is lost
fill her illness
with your presence

....
MRU

Sacred Heart of Jesus,
I place all my trust in Thee.
Sacred Heart of Jesus,
I believe in your love for me.
Sacred Heart of Jesus,
I believe you love me now.

Fr John Sullivan SJ, Servant of God

Do Not Be Afraid

Noli timere, dear breast.
God is on the case,
nursing and healing.
While sleeping,
He loves you.
While being treated,
He loves you.
Dear breast, dearly loved,
feel the power of the Father,
trust in him.

....
MRU

And there was a woman who had had a discharge of blood for twelve years, and who had suffered much under many physicians, and had spent all that she had, and was no better, but rather grew worse. She had heard the reports about Jesus, and came up behind him in the crowd and touched his garment.

For she said, 'If I but touch even his garments, I will be made well.'

And immediately the flow of blood dried up, and she felt in her body that she was healed of her disease.

And Jesus, perceiving in himself that power had gone out from him, immediately turned about in the crowd and said, 'Who touched my garments?'

And his disciples said to him, 'You see the crowd pressing around you; and yet you say, "Who touched me?"'

And he looked round to see who had done it. But the woman, knowing what had happened to her, came in fear and trembling, and fell down before him and told him the whole truth. And he said to her, 'Daughter, your faith has made you well; go in peace, and be healed of your disease.'

Mark 5:25–34

New Accessories

Mustn't forget the tea tree oil
or lavender cream
for hands and nails.
Mustn't forget the E45
for scalp and feet.
I see in the mirror
woolly white wisps
clinging to my crown.
Dear Lord, help me to discover
through this bitter cross
who I really am,
what I really believe.

....
MRU

This poem packs many powerful images into a title that seems, on the face of it, to be about trivialities.

My family's collective discovery of the importance of 'accessories' such as those in the poem, was initiated by the arrival of a package from our French sister-in-law. It arrived in a shocking week after an out-of-the-blue terminal diagnosis for our beautiful eldest brother. It contained 'exotic' potions and lotions – all organic - which seemed somehow important. These 'accessories', which were intended to build physical strength and resilience against the disease, enabled a semblance of fighting-back, which in turn enabled an assertion of control. Ultimately, they were important symbols for building resilience of spirit and mind.

I sense the same importance accruing to these matters in Mary's repeated use of the phrase "Mustn't forget [the lavender cream]..." Mustn't forget [the E45]....". They enabled many small acts of defiance against the physical intrusion of the disease on her body. The brutality of which is conveyed by the image of wisps of hair on her scalp - a very shocking and personal image for a woman who, in person, was always the epitome of physical attractiveness, grace and elegance.

The phrase 'Dear Lord...' which seems to be simultaneously both an expression of painful anguish as well as one of hopeful aspiration – leads to the poem's deceptively simple truth, unfortunately easily lost to so many of us: that knowing oneself and what one believes in, is indeed, as Mary indicates, the prize to strive for in our life – no matter what that life brings.

Deirdre Garvey, CEO of The Wheel

My Guardian Dear

O Angel of God my Guardian dear
today you prompted me
to ask about my markers.
I was overjoyed to hear
since treatment began
they have reduced by fifty per cent;
fifty per cent!
You took me off to the Oratory
where we danced, and we danced,
and we hugged.
O Angel of God my Guardian dear
to whom God's love commits me here.

....
MRU

Fever

I have brought back a good message from
the land of 102 (degrees):
God exists.
... it is truth long known
that some secrets are hidden from health.

....

John Updike

Mary probably saw in John Updike's poem 'Fever' the chance to bring comfort, which she understood to be one aspect of her own calling as a person who would choose to remain whole in illness. She told me once that she believed the ego could play a constructive role. To attempt to suppress the ego as a purely negative force was, she said, 'contrary to how life works'. Here the speaker reports back from a deep delirium, from a land beyond reason. But once returned, he is unabashed in declaring his discovery because he recognises it as a gift: beyond the conscious mind, and way beyond health, is home. What could be more comforting than that?

Sue Norton, Lecturer of English in The Dublin Institute of Technology.

Let nothing disturb thee,
Let nothing affright thee,
All things pass;
God changes not.
With patience everything is
accomplished.
Whoever has God
lacks nothing.
God alone suffices.

St Teresa of Avila's Bookmark
Translation by Mary Redmond Ussher's father, Seán Réamonn,

Thoughts

In my bay
pre-meds done, chemo on the drip
I thank God for the wonder of it all
seed of the yew nourished by
soil inhabited by earthworms
sapling sprouting to
sun and rain
sheltering insects in
maturing tree
magnificent creation's indwelling powers
of healing, rebalancing, rebodying
I thank God for the one who drew out
these powers, was she – or he – someone
fired 'to make a difference'
to extract from the ancient tree
its secrets
stewarding God's manifold gifts
so that a woman such as I might be healed

....
MRU

AFTER TREATMENT

Beginning Again

Lord God, dearest Father
take away all fears
from now on
let me be all here
return to my place and
begin again
'to be
what I already am'.*

....
MRU

*Thomas Merton OCSO

Hail, Holy Queen

Hail, Holy Queen, Mother of mercy!
Hail, our life, our sweetness and our hope!
To thee do we cry, poor banished
children of Eve: to thee do we send
up our sighs, mourning and weeping
in this valley of tears.
Turn then, most gracious advocate,
thine eyes of mercy toward us; and
after this our exile, show unto us the
blessed fruit of thy womb, Jesus.
O clement, O loving, O sweet Virgin Mary!

Amen.

The prayer Mary first utters after treatment, Hail, Holy Queen, I treasured saying as a child and years after last hearing it, I still remember - did Mary like myself love such strange, arcane expressions as banished children of Eve, valley of tears, gracious advocate, those tender eyes of mercy, and that most touching of all adjectives, clement? There is little poetry more beautiful in our language. If faith led Mary to thank and worship here, so too did her taste. Impeccable, as always.

Frank McGuinness, writer and academic.

I would like the Angels of Heaven
to be among us.
I would like an abundance of peace.
I would like full vessels of charity.
I would like rich treasures of mercy.
I would like cheerfulness to preside over all.
I would like Jesus to be present.
I would like the three Marys of illustrious
renown to be with us.
I would like the friends of Heaven
to be gathered around us from all parts.
I would like myself to be a rentpayer to the
Lord; that I should suffer distress and that
He would bestow a good blessing upon me.

Brigid of Ireland

Keep yourself at peace and in complete repose, never become upset and never trouble yourself about anything, forget the past, live as though the future does not exist, live for Jesus in every moment that you are living, or, better, live as though you have no life in yourself, but allow Jesus to live in you at His leisure.

St Francois-Marie-Jacob Libermann

Do not be anxious about your life, what you will eat or what you will drink, nor about your body, what you will put on. Is not life more than food, and the body more than clothing? Look at the birds of the air; they neither sow nor reap nor gather into barns and yet your heavenly Father feeds them.

Are you not of more value than they? And which of you by being anxious can add a single hour to his span of life? ... Therefore do not be anxious, saying, 'What shall we eat?' or 'What shall we drink?' or 'What shall we wear?'

Matthew 6:25–7, 31

We are obliged to plan for the future and take thought of tomorrow. But we should do it without worrying, without the care that gnaws at the heart but doesn't solve anything – and often prevents us from putting our hearts into what we have to do here and now. Hearts anxious about tomorrow can't be open to the grace of the present moment.

Fr Jacques Philippe

My Self

I suffer when my
would-be nothingness
advocates revisions
challenging what I really believe
illness unhinges
pro tempore obliterates
power and position
the artificial self
forgive me Father
when I find it hard
The trial of my cancer has taught me
I am a child of dust

....
MRU

I shed a tear when I first read this. Measured, sparse even in its use of words, yet so incredibly powerful.

In every line, every thought, you feel the stoicism, courage and fortitude of this extraordinary woman facing her unwanted destiny. It immediately made me think of my precious sister Anne who also faced a momentous and difficult reality, when aged just 33, and with two tiny daughters, she too was diagnosed with cancer. Her fate was sealed with drastic speed, and Anne left this world just six months after becoming ill.

Like Mary, she too faced her illness with incredible bravery. Adored by all, beautiful inside and out, heaven once again cruelly stole away the best of us. We all miss her terribly, every day.

Miriam O'Callaghan, broadcaster.

Sufficient unto the day. The things that have to be done must be done, and for the rest we must not allow ourselves to become infested with thousands of petty fears and worries, so many motions of no confidence in God.

Everything will turn out all right.

....

Etty Hillesum

This meditation points us to the essence – the blessing, even – of living with uncertainty: to allow this to direct us to the present moment, where God is. Etty Hillesum, a young Jewish woman facing death in the Holocaust, was able to find life beautiful and meaningful by obeying the gospel injunction to take no thought for the morrow. This becomes possible if we are ready to accept whatever God sends, not making our enjoyment of life conditional on a particular outcome in the future. Shakespeare inculcates this wisdom in these words: "Be absolute for death: either death or life/ Shall thereby be the sweeter."

This becomes possible through trust in Jesus. He shows us the way. His extraordinary loving gift of Himself in the Eucharist is made as He faces suffering and death. When I was facing drastic and dangerous surgery to remove a lethal cancer, I found strength and consolation in these words from the letter to the Hebrews about Him: "the pioneer and perfecter of our faith, who for the joy that was set before Him endured the cross." He faced what He had to face because the way through it was the way to joy.

Fr Luke Bell, Benedictine Monk at Quarr Abbey, Isle of Wight.

Back to Work

This week I could compare
work, the prose of everyday life
with work, the carrying of the Cross.
I found turning that prose
into heroic verse very different from
turning those thorns into roses.
God, grant me your peace.

....
MRU

"

With acknowledgment to St J. Escrivá
Peace is the simplicity of spirit, the serenity
of conscience, the tranquillity of the soul and
the bond of love.

St Pio of Pietrelcina

"

Remain at peace, my daughter. Remove from your imagination whatever may upset you and say frequently to Our Lord, 'O God, you are my God and I will trust in you; you will help me and you will be my refuge and there is nothing I will fear, because not only are you with me, but, also, you are in me and I in you.' What does a child in the arms of such a Father have to fear? Be as a little child, my dearest daughter. As you know children don't concern themselves with many matters; they have others who think for them. They are strong enough if they remain with their father. Therefore, act accordingly, my daughter, and you will be at peace.

St Francis de Sales

Not My Will

Not my will
but Yours be done.
Not this child's
but Yours, Abba.
With outstretched arms
receive me
and give me
your peace.

....
MRU

> I had no guide, no light,
> Save that which burned within my heart,
> And yet this light did guide my way,
> More surely than the noonday sun
> Unto the place where waited One
> Who knew me well.

St John of the Cross, *Canticle of the Soul*

> I have reached the stage now where I can afford to look back; in the crucible of trials from within and without, my soul has been refined, and I can raise my head like a flower after a storm and see how the words of the Psalm have been fulfilled in my case: 'The Lord is my shepherd and I shall want nothing. He hath made me to lie in pastures green and pleasant; He hath led me gently beside the waters. He hath led my soul without fatigue ... Yea, though I should go down into the valley of the shadow of death, I will fear no evil, for Thou, O Lord, art with me.'

St Thérèse of Lisieux

Peace *v.* Anxiety

Peace I seek
roots ever deepening
nourished by
the grace of God
Anxiety I spurn
plant of darkness
unbidden, sour
unwelcome

....
MRU

> **"**
>
> Cast all your anxiety on him, because he cares for you.
>
> ....
>
> 1 Peter 5:7

> **"**
>
> And we know that for those who love God all things work together for good.
>
> ....
>
> Romans 8:28

> **"**
>
> The value of persistent prayer is not that God will hear us, but that we will finally hear God.
>
> ....
>
> William J. McGill

> **"**
>
> When one door of happiness closes, another one opens, but we look so long at the closed door that we do not see the one which has been opened for us.
>
> ....
>
> Helen Keller

“

Deal bountifully with your servant,
that I may live and keep your word.

....

Psalm 119:17

“

Vultum tuum, Domine, requiram.
Your Face, O Lord, do I seek.

....

Psalm 27:8

“

Every morning, when we wake up, we have twenty-four brand new hours to live. What a precious gift!

We have the capacity to live in a way that these twenty-four hours will bring peace, joy, and happiness to ourselves and others.

Peace is present right here and now, in ourselves and in everything we do and see. ...

We can smile, breathe, walk, and eat our meals in a way that allows us to be in touch with the abundance of happiness that is available.

....

Thich Nhat Hanh

Resolutions

I pray that
old habits stay away
resolutions
made during
illness endure
may the different contour
and play of each day
become and remain
my jewels

....
MRU

May They Be

Hello scanner, my old friend
I've come to talk with you again.
Same old vision softly creeping
When awake or when I am sleeping.
And the vision that was planted
In my brain still remains –
Stable scans: survival.

....
MRU

With acknowledgement to Simon and Garfunkel,
The Sound of Silence

"

I lift up my eyes to the hills.
From where does my help come?
My help comes from the Lord,
who made heaven and earth.
He will not let your foot be moved;
he who keeps you will not slumber.
Behold, he who keeps Israel
will neither slumber nor sleep.
The Lord is your keeper;
the Lord is your shade on your right hand.
The sun shall not strike you by day,
nor the moon by night.
The Lord will keep you from all evil;
he will keep your life.
The Lord will keep
your going out and your coming in
from this time forth and for evermore.

Psalm 121

Protecting the Present

I must not allow my present
to be burdened by the weight
of the past few years
but worse would be
to allow the future's imagined weight
to burden my present.
Mary, help me to remain
at peace, to say always
to your Son
In you I trust

....
MRU

I will extol you, O Lord, for you have drawn me up
    and have not let my foes rejoice over me.
O Lord my God, I cried to you for help,
    and you have healed me. ...
You have turned for me my mourning into dancing;
    O Lord my God, I will give thanks to you for ever.

Psalm 30

AND AFTER THAT

The Canticle of Mary

My soul magnifies the Lord,
And my spirit rejoices in God my Saviour;
Because he has regarded the lowliness of his
handmaid;
For behold, henceforth all generations shall
call me blessed; because he who is mighty
has done great things for me,
and holy is his name;
And his mercy is from generation to generation
on those who fear him.
He has shown might with his arm,
he has scattered the proud in the conceit of their
heart.
He has put down the mighty from their thrones,
and has exalted the lowly.
He has filled the hungry with good things,
and the rich he has sent away empty.
He has given help to Israel, his servant,
mindful of his mercy:
Even as he spoke to our fathers,
to Abraham and to his posterity forever.

Rise up, my soul, rise up,
shake off the dust, lift yourself up,
and enter before the gaze of the Lord, your God,
to confess before him all the mercy
and compassion that he has shown to you.

Blessed are you, Adonai,
in the firmament of heaven.
Let all the marrow and
virtue of my spirit bless you.
Let all the substance
of my soul and body bless you.
Let all that is within me glorify you.

St Gertrude the Great of Helfta

Hearing the Flowers

Slow down
Don't move too fast
Want to make
Each moment last
Want to hear
The flowers grow
Feel their rhythm
In my soul

....
MRU

With acknowledgement to Simon & Garfunkel,
The 59th Street Bridge Song

One time our good Lord said:
All things shall be well;
And another time he said:
Thou shalt see thyself that all manner [of]
things shall be well.

....
Julian of Norwich

The Lord is my light and my salvation;
whom shall I fear?
The Lord is the stronghold of my life;
of whom shall I be afraid?

....
Psalm 27:1

For nothing will be impossible with God.

....
Luke 1:37

The Tandem Bike Ride

At first, I saw God as my observer, my judge, keeping track of things I did to know whether I merited heaven or hell. God was 'out there' – sort of like a president: I recognised his picture, but I did not know him.

Later on, when I met Jesus, life became a bike ride. It was a tandem bike, and Jesus was in the back helping me pedal. I don't know at what point he suggested we change places, but life has not been the same since then.

When I had the control, I knew the way. It was rather boring, but predictable. It was the shortest distance between two points. When Jesus led we took delightful longcuts – up mountains and through rocky places at breakneck speeds. It was all I could do to hang on! Even though it looked like madness, he said, 'Pedal!'

I worried and was anxious and asked, 'Where are you taking me?' He laughed, but didn't answer.

I forgot my boring life and entered into the adventure. And when I would say 'I'm scared' he'd lean back and touch my hand. He took me to people who gave me gifts of healing, acceptance, joy, and peace for our journey. He said, 'Share the gifts.' So I did – to the people we met. And I found that in giving I received, and our burden was light. I did not trust him at first to control my life. I thought he'd wreck it. But he knows how to make bikes bend and take sharp corners, jump to clear high rocks, fly to shorten scary passages. I am learning to be quiet and pedal in the strangest places. I'm beginning to enjoy the view and the cool breeze on my face. And when I'm sure I just can't do anymore, he just smiles and says, 'Pedal!'

....
Author Unknown

Inhaling the Spirit

Someone said about prayer:
'It's exhaling the spirit of man
And inhaling the spirit of God.'
I exhale the past
and inhale the present
the wondrous, life-giving present.

....
MRU

My Lord God, I have no idea where I am going.

I do not see the road ahead of me. I cannot know for certain where it will end.

Nor do I really know myself, and the fact that I think I am following your will does not mean that I am actually doing so.

But I believe that the desire to please you does in fact please you, and I hope I have that desire in all that I am doing.

And I know that if I do this, You will lead me by the right road, though I may know nothing about it.

Therefore I will trust you always though I may seem to be lost in the shadow of death.

I will not fear, for you are ever with me, and you will never leave me to face my struggle alone.

Thomas Merton OCSO

The Seasons

For most everything there is a season
A time to be told about illness
A time to take stock
A time for treatment
A time to recover
A time for re-centring
A time to glimpse hope
A time to frame plans

....
MRU

66

I call to you, O God:
Give me what I need to live!
You have good plans for me;
I may see you and know you.

....
Hildegard of Bingen

66

For surely I know the plans I have for you,
says the Lord, plans for your welfare and not
for harm, to give you a future with hope.
Then when you call upon me and come and
pray to me, I will hear you.

....
Jeremiah 29:11–12 (NRSV)

66

Fear not, for I am with you; be not dismayed,
for I am your God; I will strengthen you, I
will help you, I will uphold you with my
righteous right hand.

....
Isaiah 41:10

I

B
R
E
A
T
H
E

N O W   N O T   I

Y
O
U

B
R
E
A
T
H
E

M
E

....
MRU

"

Make a joyful noise to the Lord,
all the earth!
Serve the Lord with gladness!
Come into his presence with singing!
Know that the Lord, he is God!
It is he that made us, and we are his;
we are his people, and the sheep of his pasture.
Enter his gates with thanksgiving,
and his courts with praise!
Give thanks to him; bless his name!
For the Lord is good;
his steadfast love endures for ever,
and his faithfulness for all generations.

Psalm 100

I see His Blood upon the Rose

I see his blood upon the rose
And in the stars the glory of his eyes,
His body gleams amid eternal snows,
His tears fall from the skies.
I see his face in every flower;
The thunder and the singing of the birds
Are but his voice – and carven by his power
Rocks are his written words.
All pathways by his feet are worn,
His strong heart stirs the ever-beating sea.
His crown of thorns is twined with every thorn,
His cross is every tree.

....

Joseph Mary Plunkett

Holding Hands

Take my hand, hold it
No need to explain why you
Asked to meet, I knew by the
Quiver in your voice
Now we're sipping coffee
You tell me
That 'worrisome' tumour is malignant
You have breast cancer
Leave your hand in mine
Your colleagues never knew, you say,
Those meetings 'out of the office'
Were for cat scans, MRIs,
Lumbar punctures, mammograms,
Ultrasounds, bloods, you led
A double life until you got the news
You have breast cancer

Put both hands in mine
I can believe how devastated
Your loved ones are
Your partner's numb and wordless
Your parents and your children
Speak through tears
Your sisters and your brothers whisper
You have breast cancer
Feel the power in my hands
Know with certainty
That God is present, longing
For you to seek him
He is with you already
On your Pink Ribbon Path
Closer than ever before because
You have breast cancer

....
MRU

Thanksgiving

What can I render to the Lord
For all that he has
Rendered unto me.
For the continuing gift of life
For sparing and transforming it
I thank you.
For each new sunrise
And birdsong, your liturgy,
I thank you.
For sleeping to the gift of rest
And rising to the gift of life
I thank you.
For winter-flowering cherry blossom,
My father's rose, and lavender
I thank you.
For every cell and particle
Restored to your healing
I thank you.

For hair and nails re-grown
And new peace in my deepest core
I thank you.
For love of husband, child, mother
Siblings, spouses
I thank you.
For support of pink sisters
And tireless friends along the way
I thank you.
For nurses, doctors, their infusions
Cheery women who brought the tea
I thank you.
For every tear in near despair
The love in your Cross
I thank you.
For help in the battle
Between faith and fear
I thank you.
For having heard and answered me
Especially when I could not pray
I thank you.

For passage to a new life
Beyond all imagining
I thank you.
For new lens to discern
'success' and 'worry'
I thank you.
For Your Spirit's awesome presence
O uncreated One
I thank you.
For the music of your silence
Sweetest surrender
I thank you.
And I pray that all women
on the Pink Ribbon Path
may find and love you, Lord.
That, by your grace,
if I am again afflicted
with this disease
I may remain on the Path.
That through Mary my prayers may be
an instrument of hope;
and that one day, O God of life,
breast cancer will be overcome.

....

MRU

The Pink Ribbon Path

The Pink Ribbon Path
Is the path of the heart
Where the cry of the heart
Is heard
I will stay on this path
Walk straight in its curves
I will not be afraid
I will not be perturbed
The Pink Ribbon Path
Is the path of the heart
Where the ear of the heart
Hears You

....
MRU

LOVING MIND–BODY AWARENESS

Opening Prayer

Glory be to the Father
And to the Son
And to the Holy Spirit
O God, come to our aid.
O Lord, make haste to help us.
Holy Spirit, release in us
your healing power.
Flood our heart-room with
your loving presence,
and radiate your love
to every part of our mind and body.

Loving Mind—Body Awareness

What follows is the text of the audio exercise read by Sue Norton. Sue Norton is lecturer of English in the Dublin Institute of Technology and a freelance essayist. She is American and has lived in Ireland for many years. Sue has gifted her honorarium for this recording to Smilow Cancer Hospital (http://yalecancer-center.org/gifts/index.aspx).

Give your full body weight to where you are resting. There's nowhere to go, nothing you have to do at this time. This is a time for complete rest, unconditional love and healing. You are about to do a Loving Mind– Body Awareness. A prayer for healing. Sending loving care to every part of you, every cell and particle.

Become aware of your mind.
In this moment
lovingly let go.
Allow all tension
to fall away, seep away,
slowly.
Allow your mind
to be completely
at ease, in peace, restful.

Give thanks to your mind
for its capacity to find
a life of beauty and truth.
Send loving-kindness
to its infinite potential
for healing.

Become aware of
the deep centre of your self,
the core of your being,

from which loving kindness
flows to every part of you,
to others and
to creation.

Become aware of
your heart of love.

The love
you give and receive;
the love you have
for your self;
gentle, kind self-acceptance,
deep friendship with
every aspect of your self.

Now, become aware of your body,
resting where it is,
breathing in and
breathing out,
letting go all tension.

Lovingly turn your attention to your feet;
feel the full weight of both feet
where you are resting
from your heels to your toes.
Be aware of your ankles,

of both your legs,
coming up to your knees,
continuing on past your knees,
up the back of your thighs,
aware of both your legs easing and sinking
where you are resting.
And now coming to the base of the spine,
aware that it is heavy where it is resting.

Lovingly become aware
of your kidneys, your liver.
Let your love dwell
in the whole of your abdomen.
Continue this loving awareness
up your spine,
slowly up your spine,
through each vertebra,
bit by bit,
slowly, slowly, to the top of the spine;
coming deep down in between the shoulders,
easing and releasing the shoulders.

Send loving kindness to your breathing.
Breathing in and breathing out.
Breathing in and breathing out.
Watch the rise and fall of the breath.
The loving breath of life

as it comes in ... and flows out.
Really letting it flow out
in your very own timing.
As it comes in, really letting it flow out.
As it comes in, really letting it flow out.
And now allow the breathing to find its
own rhythm again
in the way that it wants to.

Lovingly become aware of your breasts;
your right;
your left.

Become aware of your neck
and the whole of your head,
letting the corners of your eyes really drop,
the corners of your mouth and of your jaw really drop,
allowing your whole face to soften.
Become aware of your shoulders,
your forearms, your wrists
out to the tips of your fingers,
aware of where they are resting.

Breathing in, aware of the whole body.
Breathing out, aware of the whole body.
Breathing in, calming the whole body.
Breathing out, calming the whole body.

You are ready to take up a position of
complete attention to your right arm.

Your right arm is heavy and warm;
heavy and warm.
Your left arm is heavy and warm;
heavy and warm.
Your arms are heavy and warm.

Your right leg is heavy and warm;
heavy and warm.
Your left leg is heavy and warm;
heavy and warm.
Your arms and legs are heavy and warm.

Now, gently draw a deep breath;
starting in your belly,
moving up your abdomen,
to the base of your lungs,
your upper rib cage,
your shoulders, and your neck.
Gently exhale that deep breath.
It breathes you.
Thank the Spirit for the breath of your life.

Your solar plexus is warm.
Your neck and shoulders are heavy.

Your forehead is cool and clear;
cool and clear.

Now, invite God's infinite power
to enter every pore of your body
and your mind;
slowly, slowly
suffusing every cell and particle.

Ask the Father to direct his power
to where your body needs restoring.

Feel his power going
deeper, deeper, deeper,
to that part of your body
and to your mind.

Ask the Father to bless your treatment
and to restore you
lovingly
in this present moment
and the next, and the next.

Rest peacefully in the Lord.
Breathing in;
breathing out.

When you have finished your Loving Mind–Body Awareness, take some time to raise your arms over your head, and as you do so take a deep breath in, then lower your arms slowly back to your sides, breathing out as you do so. Do this as many times as you wish. Feel revitalised in your mind and body.

Christian Meditation

On the Pink Ribbon Path try to meditate every morning and evening for at least twenty minutes and ideally for thirty.

Christian Meditation

On the Pink Ribbon Path,
in Christian Meditation,
we stand before the Lord,
watching and waiting.
In this moment and the next
we are in the presence of God.
He breathes us, dwells within,
he does not wish us to be afflicted.
Relaxed but alert,
leave everything to him.

....
MRU

Mindfulness

Christian Meditation is sometimes called Christian Mindfulness.

Mindfulness emphasises the presence of our total selves in the moment. Actually true recollection demands this too, but the full presence is too easily forgotten. ... [It demands] the awareness of one's self, the action, and the God who is there.

Presence to the moment ... means being 'all there'. ... True presence is steady, nondiscursive attention, which at the same time is relaxed and self-possessed.

[In illness we are closer*] to reality and therefore to God....Listen to these words of Karl Rahner, who puts them in the mouth of Christ: 'I am the blind alleys of all your paths, for when you no longer know how to go any further, then you have reached me.'

Ernest E. Larkin O. Carm
Extracts from article 'Christian Mindfulness'
*My insertion: MRU

In religious terms, people often talk about loving God, loving your neighbour and loving yourself. But I think only a little experience with meditating will show you that the true order is the other way round. You must first learn to be yourself and to love yourself. And secondly you must allow your neighbour to be themselves, and learn to love them. And it is then, and only then, that it makes any sense to talk about God.

Maranatha means 'come Lord' ... The essence of the mantra ... is that it brings you to silence. It is not a magic word. It is not a word that has any esoteric properties to it or anything like that. It is simply a word that is sacred in our tradition. Maranatha is possibly the oldest Christian prayer there is after the 'Our Father'. It is a word that brings us to great peacefulness, to rest and calm.

Fr John Main OSB
Extracts from The Way of Unknowing

Ma–ra–na–tha

Put equal emphasis on each syllable,
perhaps saying the mantra
as your breath rises.
Try to think the mantra, not say it.
Hear it.
Hear yourself saying it;
like a hum in the background
or a sound from far down a hill.
Every now and then you will be
distracted
just return to the mantra.
Ma–ra–na–tha

Getting Started

Choose somewhere quiet.
Sit, if you can, or lie down.
Close your eyes.
Relax your mouth, teeth and jaw.
Relax your body.
Become aware of the present moment;
its sounds, smells, touch.
Breathe gently and naturally.
Recollect that God dwells within you.
God is here;
you are home.

In Loving Memory of Mary

The Midnight Sun

For Mary Redmond

Is that her in darkness, the midnight sun?

Could she be walking An Trá Bhán at Rannafast
Hearing the famished ocean at her feet,
Administering justice to the waves,
A fair woman forgiving mistakes?

Is she the same dazzling girl,
The one who had the measure of Cambridge
Dreaming of Auden, secrets unravelling -
Kindred spirits, needing to say nothing?

Could that be her stitching the human heart
Fragile as a web, tough as spider's lace -
Having been torn, could it be repaired,
The damage done can with care be undone?

Is that her crossing a bridge in Cambridge?
Is that her forgiving waves in Rannafast?
Her veil, is it tough as spider's web?
The dazzling girl who was her own kind -

Is that her in darkness, the midnight sun?

Frank McGuinness

INDEX OF CONTRIBUTORS